Shortcut to Danish:
Beginner's Guide to Quickly Learning the Basics of the Danish Language

METTE ANDERSEN

CONTENTS

Introduction: How to Learn Danish   1

The Danish Alphabet   5

Danish Pronunciation Guide   7

Danish – English Cognates   11

Noun Genders and Plurals   15

Common Danish Nouns   19

Pronouns   21

Danish Verbs: Present and Past Tenses   25

Common Danish Verbs   29

Adjectives   31

Danish Numbers, Days and Months   33

Useful Danish Phrases   35

Glossary –Thematic Order   37

Glossary –Alphabetical Order   43

INTRODUCTION:
HOW TO LEARN DANISH

SETTING GOALS

Learning a new language is seen by many, especially English speakers, as an extremely complicated, time-consuming task and one that above a certain age is not really practical, or even possible, anymore. Learning a new language can indeed be a lot of work, but it is nowhere near impossible; in fact in many societies around the world it is the norm to speak more than one language, and sometimes several. As an English speaker you probably don't feel that you need to speak any other language and for the most part that is true. But despite this, you want to learn a new language, or are at least considering it, or you wouldn't be reading this. Learning a new language can be an extremely enriching experience and one that I feel everyone should at least honestly attempt.

What I encourage you to do is to think about what you are trying to achieve by learning Danish.

You will not learn to speak Danish so well that in a few short months you are confused for a Danish native speaker. To be frank it is unlikely this will ever happen. Instead of thinking in those kinds of terms, think about, or better yet visualize, what you want to be able to do with the language.

Do you want to get more out of a trip to Denmark? Do you want to communicate better with Danish family members? Do you want to make an effort to learn the native language of someone you love?

These are all very achievable goals.

I have written this book, not to teach you how to speak fluent Danish in one week, as that would be impossible anyways, but to give you a shortcut to the Danish language. This shortcut is achieved by focusing on the areas where Danish is similar to English and by giving you the rules of Danish, without getting hung up on the exceptions, so that you can start understanding and speaking Danish much faster than with traditional methods.

Traditional classroom methods of teaching a foreign language, like the ones you probably remember from school, can be successful with some committed students, but they can take many years to achieve results. Since what is taught in the beginning is often not very useful, if the student does not continue with the course he or she will often remember very little. In contrast to that approach this book will give you an extremely useful introduction to the Danish language. After completing this book it will be up to you if you continue to learn the language, but even if you go no further than this guide, the basic building blocks of the Danish language that you will have learned from this book will be useful in the future and bring you closer to your Danish language goals.

TAKE ADVANTAGE OF ONLINE TOOLS

The internet age has forever changed our approach to language learning. It is now easy, with no more than a quick Google search and a few clicks of the mouse, to listen to Danish radio, watch a Danish comedy or read the news in Danish. In addition to media for native speakers, there is a seemingly never-ending supply of material to learn almost any new language.

Two tools that I recommend to complement this book are:

forvo.com
A language book like this one can be a great introduction to a new language. As adults we crave explanations as to why the language works the way it does and try to find the underlying "rules" or "patterns" and books like this are useful to give these explanations. The major downside to language books of course is that you cannot hear the language spoken. Forvo solves this problem.

Go to forvo.com and type in any Danish word in this book and immediately hear it pronounced by a native speaker!

Anki

It has been said that repetition is the mother of all learning, and when it comes to learning vocabulary it is hard to argue with this logic. Anki is a spaced-repetition flashcard program that you can install on a computer or as an app on your smartphone or tablet. Make flashcards of the Danish words you want to memorize and Anki will decide when you need to see that word next in order to efficiently memorize it.

It is my sincere hope that this book proves useful to you and helps you achieve your Danish language goals.

THE DANISH ALPHABET

The Danish language uses the same Latin alphabet as English, but with the addition of 3 new letters after the z. The letters with their names in Danish are given in the table below:

Danish Letter	Danish Name
a	a
b	be
c	se
d	de
e	e
f	æf
g	ge
h	hå
i	i
j	jåd
k	kå
l	æl
m	æm
n	æn
o	o

p	pe
q	ku
r	ær
s	æs
t	te
u	u
v	ve
w	dobbelt-ve
x	æks
y	y
z	sæt
æ	æ
ø	ø
å	å

DANISH PRONUNCIATION GUIDE

Pronunciation is one of the most difficult aspects of the Danish language and the relationship between the written word and the spoken word is not always clear. Danish has many silent letters and a few strange sounds that make it difficult to achieve correct pronunciation for a non-Dane.

Danish pronunciation is even the butt of jokes within Scandinavia, with the Swedes saying that Danes speak as if they have a hot potato in their mouths, and a Norwegian comedy program called "Uti Vår Hage" going so far as to claim that actually Danes cannot even understand each other!

Below is a rough guide to reading words in Danish. Despite these guidelines it is common to find words that break these "rules" and spoken Danish does not always closely resemble the written word. This is unfortunately just something that you have to get used to, but with practice, it does get easier.

Danish Letter	Pronunciation Guideline
a	"e" as in egg or "a" as in father
b	"b" as in beer word-initially; "w" as in win when word-final or between vowels
c	"k" as in kite before a consonant, a, o, or u; "s" as in sea elsewhere

d	"**d**" as in **d**og word-initially; "soft d" when final or between vowels. This sound is somewhat like the "**th**" as in **th**is but sounds almost like an "**l**" to English speakers; after l, n or r or before s or t it is usually silent
e	"**a**" as in **a**che or "**e**" as in b**e**d or "**e**" as in **o**pen
f	"**f**" as in **f**eet
g	"**g**" as in **g**ood; after vowels it is rarely pronounced
h	"**h**" as in **h**is; silent before j or v
i	"**ee**" as in b**ee**
j	"**y**" as in **y**es
k	"**k**" as in **k**ick word-initially; "**g**" as in **g**et between vowels or word-final
l	"**l**" as in **l**ight
m	"**m**" as in **m**eat
n	"**n**" as in **n**et
o	"**o**" as in **o**ld or "**o**" as in c**o**t
p	"**p**" as in **p**ie word-initially; "**b**" as in **b**ite between vowels and word-final
q	similar to English

r	"**r**" as in the French **r**ue word-initially; after a vowel it "colors" the vowel sound or is silent
s	always "**s**" as in **s**it; never with a "z" sound like in hou**s**es
t	"**t**" as in **t**en word-initially; "**d**" as in **d**oor between vowels; same as "soft d" at the end of a word
u	"**oo**" as in t**oo**th
v	"**v**" as in **v**an word-initially; "**oo**" as in b**oo**t between vowels or word-final
w	"**v**" as in **v**an
x	"**x**" as in ta**x**i
y	"**u**" as in c**u**te but with lips more rounded. Same as the French "u" or German "ü"
z	"**s**" as in **s**et
æ	"**e**" as in b**e**d or "**a**" as in **a**rt
ø	"**ir**" as in th**ir**st but shorter. Same as the German ö
å	"**o**" as in c**o**t or "**o**" as in **o**ld

DANISH–ENGLISH COGNATES

Danish and English are closely related languages that share a lot of their core vocabulary. This includes:

ANIMALS

kat – cat
fisk – fish
mus – mouse
ko – cow
lam – lamb

PARTS OF THE BODY

arm – arm
finger – finger
knæ – knee
fod – foot
hår – hair

HOUSEHOLD ITEMS

hus – house
dør – door
kniv – knife

FAMILY MEMBERS

moder – mother (usually shortened to **mor**)
fader – father (usually shortened to **far**)
broder – brother (usually shortened to **bror**)
søster – sister
søn – son
datter – daughter

SIMPLE VERBS

drikke – drink
kysse – kiss
finde – find
gå – go
kan – can (be able to)

As an English speaker these cognates are very helpful and make learning the Danish language much easier than learning an unrelated language. Pay attention to words that are cognates but do not have the exact same meaning in English as in Danish. For example **hund** in Danish is "dog" and not just a hunting dog like the English word "hound". There are also some false-cognates (or "false-friends"), i.e. words that look similar but whose meanings are not the same. A famous example is the Danish word **gift**, which means either "poison" or "marriage" but never "gift"!

In addition to basic vocabulary, the grammar of Danish has a lot in common with the grammar of English.

The word order is largely the same:

Du kan drikke kaffe med mælk.
You can drink coffee with milk.

Kan jeg sidde her?
Can I sit here?

There are no case declensions in Danish except for the genitive (possessive form), which adds an –s ending in a similar way to English.

en pige
a girl

en piges hus
a girl's house (no apostrophe in Danish)

Danish and English have similar systems of "weak" verbs and "strong" verbs. Like in English, "weak" verbs add a –d or –t sound in the past tense and are largely regular, whereas "strong" verbs change vowel sounds in the past tense and are irregular. For example:

Weak verb
jeg kysser – jeg kyssede – jeg har kysset
I kiss – I kissed – I have kissed

Strong verb
vi synger – vi sang – vi har sunget
we sing – we sang – we have sung

The structure of Danish is in many ways similar to that of English, and this is a real advantage to learning Danish as an English speaker.

Unfortunately the pronunciation is not as similar as the grammar is!

NOUN GENDERS AND PLURALS

GENDER

Like most European languages, but unlike English, Danish nouns have grammatical gender. Unlike French and Spanish that have masculine and feminine genders, Danish nouns are grouped into either common or neuter genders. The distribution of nouns into genders is largely arbitrary and the gender of a noun must therefore be memorized alongside the noun. Approximately 75% of nouns are common gender, so if you don't know a noun's gender, common is your best guess.

The gender of the noun determines the articles that are used with that noun. The word for "a/an" in Danish is **en** for common gender nouns and **et** for neuter nouns. For this reason common nouns are often called **en** nouns, and neuter nouns called **et** nouns.

en dreng – en pige
a boy – a girl

et hus – et æble
a house – an apple

The words for "the" is Danish use the same form as the words for "a/an" but the **en** or **et** is moved to the end of the word. If the word already ends in an "e", then only **n** or **t** is added.

drengen – pigen
the boy – the girl

huset – æblet
the house – the apple

15

PLURALS

The most common way to form plurals in Danish is to add an –e or an –er to the end of the singular form. There is no hard and fast rule about which ending to use, but there are some trends. The –er ending is the most common, and multi–syllable words usually take the –er ending. Nouns which take the –e ending are often single syllable, common gender words. Singular forms that end in –e, e.g. **pige** "girl", often add –r to form the plural. In addition to this system, there are words that do not change in the plural (like the English "deer"), and words that have irregular plurals (like the English "child – children").

en dreng – drenge
a boy – boys

en pige – piger
a girl – girls

et hus – huse
a house – houses

et æble – æbler
an apple – apples

Note that if the singular form ends in a stressed short vowel followed by a consonant, the consonant is doubled in the plural. This is done merely to preserve the pronunciation and is similar to English. For example:

en bus – busser
a bus – busses

To add the definite article to the plural form, in Danish you add –
ne to the –**er** or the –**e** ending. Irregular plural nouns that do not
add –**e** or –**er** often add –**ene** to the plural form.

en dreng – drengen – drenge – drengene
a boy – the boy – boys – the boys

en pige – pigen – piger – pigerne
a girl – the girl – girls – the girls

et hus – huset – huse – husene
a house – the house – houses – the houses

et æble – æblet – æbler – æblerne
an apple – the apple – apples – the apples

COMMON DANISH NOUNS

Below is a list of common Danish nouns. The plural form is given in parentheses. Note that some nouns do not have a plural form in Danish.

ANIMALS

et dyr (dyr) – an animal (animals)
en hund (hunde) – a dog (dogs)
en kat (katte) – a cat (cats)
en fisk (fisk) – a fish (fish)
en fugl (fugle) – a bird (birds)
en ko (køer) – a cow (cows)
et svin (svin) – a pig (pig)
en mus (mus) – a mouse (mice)
en hest (heste) – a horse (horses)

PEOPLE

en person (personer) – a person (people)
en mor (mødre) – a mother (mothers)
en far (fædre) – a father (fathers)
en søn (sønner) – a son (sons)
en datter (døtre) – a daughter (daughters)
en bror (brødre) – a brother (brothers)
en søster (søstre) – a sister (sisters)
en mand (mænd) – a man (men)
en kvinde (kvinder) – a woman (women)
en dreng (drenge) – a boy (boys)
en pige (piger) – a girl (girls)
et barn (børn) – a child (children)
en ven (venner) – a friend (friends)

PARTS OF THE BODY

en krop (kroppe) – a body (bodies)
et hoved (hoveder) – a head (heads)
et ansigt (ansigter) – a face (faces)
et hår (hår) – a hair (hairs)
et øje (øjne) – an eye (eyes)
en mund (munde) – a mouth (mouths)
en næse (næser) – a nose (noses)
et øre (ører) – an ear (ears)
en hånd (hænder) – a hand (hands)
en arm (arme) – an arm (arms)
en fod (fødder) – a foot (feet)
et ben (ben) – a leg (legs)
et hjerte (hjerter) – a heart (hearts)
et blod – blood
en knogle (knogler) – a bone (bones)
et skæg (skæg) – a beard (beards)

FOOD & DRINK

en mad – food
et kød – meat
et brød (brød) – bread (breads)
en ost (oste) – cheese (cheeses)
et æble (æbler) – apple (apples)
et vand (vande) – water
et øl (øl) – beer
en vin (vine) – wine (wines)
en kaffe – coffee
en te (teer) – tea (teas)
en mælk – milk

PRONOUNS

Danish pronouns are very similar to English. The subject pronouns are:

jeg – I (**jeg** rhymes with "die").
du – you
han – he
hun – she
den / det – it
vi – we
I – you (plural) (I is pronounced "ee")
de – they (**de** is pronounced "dee")

Note that there are two forms for "it". These two forms correspond to the two genders, **den** for **en** words and **det** for **et** words. Also note that Danish has a plural form of "you" used when speaking to more than one person. Standard English does not have this form but some regional forms exist, such as "y'all". Remember that the Danish **I** (pronounced "ee") means "you" and not the same as the English "I".

Just like in English, Danish has a different set of object pronouns (the difference between "I" and "me" in English). The object pronouns are:

mig – me (**mig** sounds like "my")
dig – you (**dig** sound like "die")
ham – him
hende – her
den / det – it
os – us
jer – you (plural)
dem – them

Jeg elsker dig
I love you

Du elsker mig
You love me

Han elsker hende
He loves her

Hun elsker ham
She loves him

Danish also has a set of possessive pronouns that correspond to the English "my", "your" etc. The possessive pronouns are:

min / mit / mine – my / mine
din / dit / dine – your / yours
hans – his
hendes – her
dens / dets – its
vores – our / ours
jeres – your (plural) / yours (plural)
deres – their / theirs

There are two important things to notice about this list. One is that the forms for "my" and "your" change depending on the noun. This corresponds to the **en** and **et** genders. For **en** words, use the form that ends in –n, for **et** words use the form that ends in –t, and for all plurals use the –**ne** form.

min arm
my arm

mit hår
my hair

dine heste
your horses

22

The other important thing is that the possessive pronouns in Danish are used for both the possessive pronouns and the possessive adjectives, meaning that the same word is used for the English "my" and "mine".

min hund
my dog

hunden er min
the dog is mine

DANISH VERBS:
PRESENT AND PAST TENSES

PRESENT TENSE

This is where Danish gets easy!

Conjugating verbs is one way where Danish is simpler than most European languages including English. In Danish verbs do not change form for person or number, meaning that in any given tense there is only a single form of the verb and there are no exceptions.

To illustrate this let's look at three verbs: "to be", "to have" and "to crawl". Notice that there are various different forms in English, but there is only a single form in Danish:

jeg er – I am
du er – you are
hun er – she is
vi er – we are
I er – you (plural) are
de er – they are

jeg har – I have
du har – you have
hun har – she has
vi har – we have
I har – you (plural) have
de har – they have

jeg kravler – I crawl
du kravler – you crawl
han kravler – he crawls
vi kravler – we crawl
I kravler – you (plural) crawl
de kravler – they crawl

As you can see this is simpler than English and much simpler than languages like Spanish and Italian that have a different form for each person.

To negate verbs you simply add **ikke** after the verb:

han kravler ikke
he does not crawl

PAST TENSE

Just like English, Danish has two past tense forms, called "weak verbs" and "strong verbs". The weak verbs, also called "regular verbs", in English are verbs that simply add a –d or –ed ending to form the past tense, such as walk – walked, admire – admired, escape – escaped etc.

The most common type of verb in Danish adds **–ede** to the basic form of the verb to make the past tense. This is the form you can assume if you have not yet learned the proper past tense form. As in the present tense, the same form of the verb is used regardless of person.

jeg arbejder – **jeg arbejdede**
I work – I worked

du spiller – **du spillede**
you play – you played

Some weak verbs in Danish add –te to the stem of the verb instead of –ede to form the past tense.

vi spiser – vi spiste
we eat – we ate

de kører – de kørte
they drive – they drove

Danish strong verbs involve a vowel change to the stem in order to form the past tense. This corresponds to English irregular verbs such as drink – drank, run – ran, fly – flew. Like in English the strong verbs in Danish are irregular and there is no general rule that can be learned as a shortcut. The number of Danish strong verbs is quite small, but many are high frequency words that are used all the time. Many verbs that are irregular in English are also irregular in Danish, such as:

jeg giver dig
I give you

du gav mig
you gave me

hun gå
she goes

han gik
he went

COMMON DANISH VERBS

Below is a list of common verbs in Danish, listed with the infinitive, the present tense form and the past tense form. Note that many common verbs are similar to English.

være – **er** – **var** – to be
have – **har** – **havde** – to have
gøre – **gør** – **gjorde** – to do
sige – **siger** – **sadge** – to say
snakke – **snakker** – **snakkede** – to speak
se – **ser** – **så** – to see
gå – **går** – **gik** – to go / to walk
løbe – **løber** – **løb** – to run
springe – **springer** – **sprang** – to jump
arbejde – **arbejder** – **arbejdede** – to work
lege – **leger** – **legede** – to play
flyve – **flyver** – **fløj** – to fly
svømme – **svømmer** – **svømmede** – to swim
spise – **spiser** – **spiste** – to eat
drikke – **drikker** – **drak** – to drink
lave – **laver** – **lavede** – to cook
grine – **griner** – **grinte** – to laugh
græde – **græder** – **græd** – to cry
sidde – **sidder** – **sad** – to sit
stå – **står** – **stod** – to stand
elske – **esker** – **elskede** – to love
hade – **hader** – **hadede** – to hate
kysse – **kysser** – **kyssede** – to kiss
danse – **danser** – **dansede** – to dance
sove – **sover** – **sov** – to sleep
synge – **synger** – **sang** – to sing
lære – **lærer** – **lærte** – to learn
tænke – **tænker** – **tænkte** – to think

læse – **læser** – **læste** – to read
skrive – **skriver** – **skrev** – to write
åbne – **åbner** – **åbnede** – to open
lukke – **lukker** – **lukkede** – to close
købe – **køber** – **købte** – to buy
betale – **betaler** – **betalte** – to pay
sælge – **sælger** – **solgte** – to sell

ADJECTIVES

Adjectives in Danish inflect for gender and number, meaning they have different forms depending on whether the noun is an **en** noun or an **et** noun and also whether the noun is singular or plural.

As we have already seen, when you want to say "the dog" or "the house", the **en** or **et** that corresponds to the gender of the noun is added to the end of the word for the singular and for the plural – **ne** is added to the end of the plural form of the noun.

hunden
the dog

huset
the house

husene
the houses

If you want to add an adjective to this phrase and say "the big dog", the word "the" is removed from the noun and brought before the adjective like in English, but a different word is used.

den store hund
the big dog

det store hus
the big house

de store huse
the big houses

Notice that the word for "the" changes depending if the noun is an **en** word, an **et** word, or a plural. The word for "big" in Danish is **stor**, however between "the" and the noun an –**e** is added in each case to make **store**. If instead you want to say "a big dog" it is a little more complicated. In this case there are three forms of the adjective depending again on the gender and number of the noun. The three forms are as follows:

en stor hund
a big dog

et stort hus
a big house

store huse
big houses

The three forms of the adjective are: no ending for **en** nouns, –**t** for **et** nouns and –**e** for plural nouns. The same three forms are used if instead of "a big dog" you want to say "the dog is big".

hunden er stor
the dog is big

huset er stort
the house is big

husene er store
the houses are big

This is the basic pattern in Danish for all adjectives; however there are exceptions that have to be learned on a case by case basis.

DANISH NUMBERS, DAYS AND MONTHS

NUMBERS

en – one
to – two
tre – three
fire – four
fem – five
seks – six
syv – seven
otte – eight
ni – nine
ti – ten
ellevte – eleven
tolvte – twelve
tretten – thirteen
fjorten – fourteen
femtende – fifteen
seksten – sixteen
sytten – seventeen
atten – eighteen
nitten – nineteen
tyve – twenty
tredive – thirty
fyrre – forty
halvtreds – fifty
tres – sixty
halvfjerds – seventy
firs – eighty
halvfems – ninety
et hundrede – one hundred
et tusind – one thousand

DAYS OF THE WEEK

mandag – Monday
tirsdag – Tuesday
onsdag – Wednesday
torsdag – Thursday
fredag – Friday
lørdag – Saturday
søndag – Sunday

MONTHS OF THE YEAR

januar – January
februar – February
marts – March
april – April
maj – May
juni – June
juli – July
august – August
september – September
oktober – October
november – November
december – December

USEFUL DANISH PHRASES

Hej
Hi

Hvordan har du det?
How are you?

Godt, tak.
Fine, thank you

Ja
Yes

Nej
No

Hvad hedder du?
What is your name?

Jeg hedder Rasmus.
My name is Rasmus.

Det var hyggeligt at møde dig.
Nice to meet you.

Hvor er du fra?
Where are you from?

Jeg kommer fra Danmark.
I am from Denmark

God morgen
Good morning

God eftermiddag
Good afternoon

God aften
Good evening

God nat
Good night

Farvel
Good bye

Undskyld
Excuse me

Vær så venlig
Please

Tak
Thank you

Det forstår jeg ikke.
I don't understand

Jeg ved ikke
I don't know

Snakker du engelsk?
Do you speak English?

Snakker du dansk?
Do you speak Danish?

Ja, en smule.
Yes, a little.

Jeg snakker ikke godt dansk
I don't speak Danish well

GLOSSARY – THEMATIC ORDER

ANIMALS

dyr (–et, dyr)	animal
hund (–en, –e)	dog
kat (–ten, –te)	cat
fisk (–en, fisk)	fish
fugl (–en, –e)	bird
ko (–en, køer)	cow
svin (–et, svin)	pig
mus (–en, mus)	mouse
hest (–en, –e)	horse

PEOPLE

person (–en, –er)	person
mor (–en, mødre)	mother
far (–en, fædre)	father
søn (–nen, –ner)	son
datter (–en, døtre)	daughter
bror (–en, brødre)	brother
søster (–en, søstre)	sister
ven (–nen, –ner)	friend
mand (–en, mænd)	man
kvinde (–n, –r)	woman
dreng (–en, –e)	boy
pige (–n, –r)	girl
barn (–et, børn)	child

LOCATION

by (–en, –er)	city
hus (–et, e)	house
gade (–n, –r)	street
lufthavn (–en, –e)	airport
hotel (–let, –ler)	hotel
restaurant (–en, –er)	restaurant
skole (–n, –r)	school
universitet (–et, –er)	university
park (–en, –er)	park
butik (–en, –er)	store / shop
hospital (–et, –er)	hospital
kirke (–n, –r)	church
land (–et, –e)	country (state)
bank (–en, –er)	bank
marked (–et, –er)	market

HOME

bord (–et, –e)	table
stol (–en, –e)	chair
vindue (–t, –r)	window
dør (–en, –e)	door
bog (–en, bøger)	book

CLOTHING

tøj (–et, –er)	clothing
hat (–ten, –te)	hat
kjole (–n, –r)	dress
skjorte (–n, –r)	shirt
bukser (–en)	pants
sko (–en, sko)	shoe

BODY

krop (–pen, –pe)	body
hoved (–et, –er)	head
ansigt (–et, –er)	face
hår (–et, hår)	hair
øje (–t, øjne)	eye
mund (–en, –e)	mouth
næse (–n, –r)	nose
øre (–t, –r)	ear
hånd (–en, hænder)	hand
arm (–en, –e)	arm
fod (–en, fødder)	foot
ben (–et, ben)	leg
hjerte (–t, –r)	heart
blod (–et)	blood
knogle (–n, –r)	bone
skæg (–get, skæg)	beard

MISCELLANEOUS

ja	yes
nej	no

FOOD & DRINK

mad (–en)	food
kød (–et)	meat
brød (–et, brød)	bread
ost (–en, –e)	cheese
æble (–t, –r)	apple
vand (–et, –e)	water
øl (–let, øl)	beer
vin (–en, –e)	wine
kaffe (–n)	coffee
te (–en, –er)	tea
mælk (–en)	milk

morgenmad (–en)	breakfast
frokost (–en)	lunch
aftenmad (–en)	dinner

COLORS

farve (–n, –r)	color
rød (–t, –e)	red
blå (–t, blå)	blue
grøn (–t, –ne)	green
gul (–t, –e)	yellow
sort (sort, –e)	black
hvid (–t, –e)	white

NATURE

hav (–et, –e)	sea
flod (–en, –er)	river
sø (–en, –er)	lake
bjerg (–et, –e)	mountain
regn (–en)	rain
sne (–en)	snow
træ (–et, –er)	tree
blomst (–en, –er)	flower
sol (–en, –e)	sun
måne (–n, –r)	moon
vind (–en, –e)	wind
himmel (–en, himle)	sky
ild (–en)	fire
is (–en, is)	ice

COMMON VERBS

være (er, var)	to be
have (har , havde)	to have
gøre (gør, gjorde)	to do
sige (–r, sadge)	to say
snakke (–r, –de)	to speak
se (–r, så)	to see
gå (–r, gik)	to go / to walk
løbe (–r, løb)	to run
springe (–r, sprang)	to jump
arbejde (–r, –de)	to work
lege (–r, –de)	to play
flyve (–r, fløj)	to fly
svømme (–r, –de)	to swim
spise (–r, spiste)	to eat
drikke (–r, drak)	to drink
lave (–r, –de)	to cook
grine (–r, grinte)	to laugh
græde (–r, græd)	to cry
sidde (–r, sad)	to sit
stå (–r, stod)	to stand
elske (–r, –de)	to love
hade (–r, –de)	to hate
kysse (–r, –de)	to kiss
danse (–r, –de)	to dance
sove (–r, sov)	to sleep
synge (–r, sang)	to sing
lære (–r, lærte)	to learn
tænke (–r, tænkte)	to think
læse (–r, læste)	to read
skrive (–r, skrev)	to write
åbne (–r, –de)	to open
lukke (–r, –de)	to close
købe (–r, købte)	to buy
betale (–r, betalte)	to pay
sælge (–r, solgte)	to sell

ADJECTIVES

stor (–t, –e)	big
lille (lille, små)	small
god (–t, –e)	good
dårlig (–t, –e)	bad
varm (–t, –e)	hot
kold (–t, –e)	cold
billig (–t, –e)	cheap
dyr (–t, –e)	expensive
glad (glad, –e)	happy
trist (trist, –e)	sad

TIME

dag (–en, –e)	day
måned (–en, –er)	month
år (–et, år)	year
time (–n, –r)	hour
i dag	today
i morgen	tomorrow
i går	yesterday

SEASONS

sommer (–en, somre)	summer
efterår (–et, efterår)	fall
vinter (–en, vintre)	winter
forår (–et, forår)	spring

GLOSSARY – ALPHABETICAL ORDER

A

aftenmad (–en)	dinner
ansigt (–et, –er)	face
april	April
arbejde (–r, –de)	work
arm (–en, –e)	arm
atten	eighteen
august	August

B

bank (–en, –er)	bank
barn (–et, børn)	child
ben (–et, ben)	leg
betale (–r, betalte)	pay
billig (–t, –e)	cheap
bjerg (–et, –e)	mountain
blod (–et)	blood
blomst (–en, –er)	flower
blå (–t, blå)	blue
bog (–en, bøger)	book
bord (–et, –e)	table
bror (–en, brødre)	brother
brød (–et, brød)	bread
bukser (–en)	pants
butik (–en, –er)	store / shop
by (–en, –er)	city

D

dag (–en, –e)	day
danse (–r, –de)	dance
datter (–en, døtre)	daughter
dårlig (–t, –e)	bad
december	December
dreng (–en, –e)	boy
drikke (–r, drak)	drink
dyr (–et, dyr)	animal
dyr (–t, –e)	expensive
dør (–en, –e)	door

E

efterår (–et, efterår)	fall
ellevte	eleven
elske (–r, –de)	love
en	one

F

far (–en, fædre)	father
farve (–n, –r)	color
februar	February
fem	five
femtende	fifteen
fire	four
firs	eighty
fisk (–en, fisk)	fish
fjorten	fourteen
flod (–en, –er)	river
flyve (–r, fløj)	fly
fod (–en, fødder)	foot
forår (–et, forår)	spring
fredag	Friday
frokost (–en)	lunch

44

fugl (–en, –e)	bird
fyrre	forty

G

gade (–n, –r)	street
glad (glad, –e)	happy
god (–t, –e)	good
grine (–r, grinte)	laugh
græde (–r, græd)	cry
grøn (–t, –ne)	green
gul (–t, –e)	yellow
gøre (gør, gjorde)	do
gå (–r, gik)	go / walk

H

hade (–r, –de)	hate
halvfems	ninety
halvfjerds	seventy
halvtreds	fifty
hat (–ten, –te)	hat
hav (–et, –e)	sea
have (har , havde)	have
hest (–en, –e)	horse
himmel (–en, himle)	sky
hjerte (–t, –r)	heart
hospital (–et, –er)	hospital
hotel (–let, –ler)	hotel
hoved (–et, –er)	head
hund (–en, –e)	dog
hundrede	hundred
hus (–et, e)	house
hvid (–t, –e)	white
hånd (–en, hænder)	hand
hår (–et, hår)	hair

I

i dag	today
i går	yesterday
i morgen	tomorrow
ild (–en)	fire
is (–en, is)	ice

J

ja	yes
januar	January
juli	July
juni	June

K

kaffe (–n)	coffee
kat (–ten, –te)	cat
kirke (–n, –r)	church
kjole (–n, –r)	dress
knogle (–n, –r)	bone
ko (–en, køer)	cow
kold (–t, –e)	cold
krop (–pen, –pe)	body
kvinde (–n, –r)	woman
kysse (–r, –de)	kiss
købe (–r, købte)	buy
kød (–et)	meat

L

land (–et, –e)	country (state)
lave (–r, –de)	cook
lege (–r, –de)	play
lille (lille, små)	small

lufthavn (–en, –e)	airport
lukke (–r, –de)	close
lære (–r, lærte)	learn
læse (–r, læste)	read
løbe (–r, løb)	run
lørdag	Saturday

M

mad (–en)	food
maj	May
mand (–en, mænd)	man
mandag	Monday
marked (–et, –er)	market
marts	March
mor (–en, mødre)	mother
morgenmad (–en)	breakfast
mund (–en, –e)	mouth
mus (–en, mus)	mouse
mælk (–en)	milk
måne (–n, –r)	moon
måned (–en, –er)	month

N

nej	no
ni	nine
nitten	nineteen
november	November
næse (–n, –r)	nose

O

oktober	October
onsdag	Wednesday
ost (–en, –e)	cheese
otte	eight

P

park (–en, –er)	park
person (–en, –er)	person
pige (–n, –r)	girl

R

regn (–en)	rain
restaurant (–en, –er)	restaurant
rød (–t, –e)	red

S

se (–r, så)	see
seks	six
seksten	sixteen
september	September
sidde (–r, sad)	sit
sige (–r, sadge)	say
skjorte (–n, –r)	shirt
sko (–en, sko)	shoe
skole (–n, –r)	school
skrive (–r, skrev)	write
skæg (–get, skæg)	beard
snakke (–r, –de)	speak
sne (–en)	snow
sol (–en, –e)	sun
sommer (–en, somre)	summer

sort (sort, –e)	black
sove (–r, sov)	sleep
spise (–r, spiste)	eat
springe (–r, sprang)	jump
stol (–en, –e)	chair
stor (–t, –e)	big
stå (–r, stod)	stand
svin (–et, svin)	pig
svømme (–r, –de)	swim
synge (–r, sang)	sing
sytten	seventeen
syv	seven
sælge (–r, solgte)	sell
sø (–en, –er)	lake
søn (–nen, –ner)	son
søndag	Sunday
søster (–en, søstre)	sister

T

te (–en, –er)	tea
ti	ten
time (–n, –r)	hour
tirsdag	Tuesday
to	two
tolvte	twelve
torsdag	Thursday
tre	three
træ (–et, –er)	tree
tredive	thirty
tres	sixty
tretten	thirteen
trist (trist, –e)	sad
tusind	thousand
tyve	twenty
tænke (–r, tænkte)	think
tøj (–et, –er)	clothing

U

universitet (–et, –er)	university

V

vand (–et, –e)	water
varm (–t, –e)	hot
ven (–nen, –ner)	friend
vin (–en, –e)	wine
vind (–en, –e)	wind
vindue (–t, –r)	window
vinter (–en, vintre)	winter
være (er, var)	be

Æ

æble (–t, –r)	apple

Ø

øje (–t, øjne)	eye
øl (–let, øl)	beer
øre (–t, –r)	ear

Å

åbne (–r, –de)	open
år (–et, år)	year

Made in the USA
Middletown, DE
13 July 2017